PRO FOOTBALL'S
STARS OF THE
DEFENSE

by Michael Sandler

Consultant: Norries Wilson
Head Football Coach
Columbia University

BEARPORT
PUBLISHING

New York, New York

Credits
Cover and Title Page C, © PCN Photography/Alamy Cover and Title Page L, © AP Images/
David Stluka; Cover and Title Page R, © Rob Tringali/Sportschrome/Getty Images;
TOCL, © Joe Robbins/Getty Images; TOCR, © Michael Democker/The Times-Picayune/
Landov; 4, © Newman Lowrance/Getty Images; 5T, © Chris Graythen/Getty Images; 5B,
© Jed Jacobsohn/Getty Images; 6, © AP Images/NFL Photos; 7, © Marcus Chacona/UPI/
Newscom; 8, © NFL Photos/Getty Images; 9, © AP Images/Tom Olmscheid; 10, © NFL
Photos/Getty Images; 11, © Chad Ryan/CSM/Landov; 12, © NFL Photos/Getty Images; 13,
© AP Images/Chris Schneider; 14, © NFL Photos/Getty Images; 15, © Michael Zagaris/
Getty Images; 16, © NFL Photos/Getty Images; 17, © Joe Robbins/Getty Images; 18, ©
NFL Photos/Getty Images; 19, © Matt Sullivan/Getty Images; 20, © NFL Photos/Getty
Images; 21, © Michael Democker/The Times-Picayune/Landov; 22L, © Joe Robbins/Getty
Images; 22R, © Michael Democker/The Times-Picayune/Landov.

Publisher: Kenn Goin
Senior Editor: Lisa Wiseman
Creative Director: Spencer Brinker
Design: Keith Plechaty
Photo Researcher: Picture Perfect Professionals, LLC

Library of Congress Cataloging-in-Publication Data

Sandler, Michael.
  Pro football's stars of the defense / by Michael Sandler ; consultant, Norries Wilson.
    p. cm. — (Football-o-rama)
  Includes bibliographical references and index.
  ISBN-13: 978-1-936088-25-6 (library binding)
  ISBN-10: 1-936088-25-8 (library binding)
  1. Football—Defense. 2. National Football League. I. Title.
GV951.18.S26 2011
796.332'2—dc22
                           2010014985

For more information, write to Bearport Publishing Company, Inc., 101 Fifth Avenue, Suite
6R, New York, New York 10003. Printed in the United States of America in North Mankato,
Minnesota.

072010
042110CGF

10 9 8 7 6 5 4 3 2 1

CONTENTS

STARS OF THE DEFENSE

For NFL teams, scoring points is only half the game. Great **defense** is just as important for a win.

The league's greatest defenses are built around star players who excel at their jobs. By stopping the run and shutting down the pass, these defensive players make it nearly impossible for the other team to gain yards or score points.

San Francisco 49ers linebacker Patrick Willis (#52) sacks quarterback Kyle Boller (#12) of the St. Louis Rams.

This book features the talented athletes who play at the different defensive positions. You will learn about **linebackers** such as Elvis Dumervil and Patrick Willis, who put nonstop pressure on the quarterbacks. You will meet **cornerbacks** and **safeties** such as Darren Sharper, Darrelle Revis, and Charles Woodson, who keep **receivers** from catching passes. You will also discover the powerful players of the **defensive line** such as Jared Allen, Dwight Freeney, and Haloti Ngata. Each one is a star of the defense!

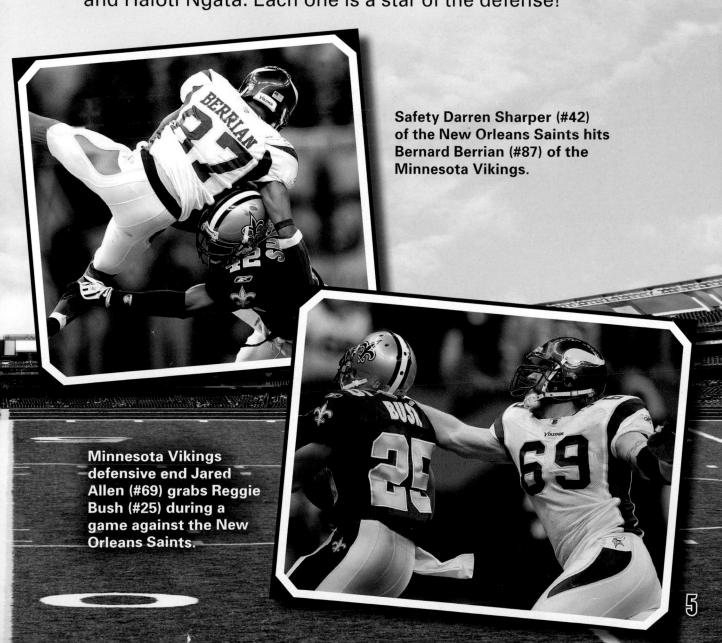

Safety Darren Sharper (#42) of the New Orleans Saints hits Bernard Berrian (#87) of the Minnesota Vikings.

Minnesota Vikings defensive end Jared Allen (#69) grabs Reggie Bush (#25) during a game against the New Orleans Saints.

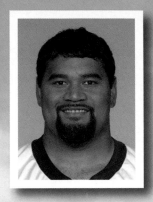

HALOTI NGATA #92
BALTIMORE RAVENS

Position: Defensive Tackle
Born: 1/21/1984 in Inglewood, California
Height: 6' 4" (1.93 m)

Weight: 345 pounds (156 kg)
College: Oregon
Pro Bowls: 1

Defensive tackles aren't as flashy as cornerbacks or linebackers. They usually do boring things such as clog up the middle of the field, tackle **running backs**, and keep blockers busy.

That's why, in September 2006, the Baltimore Ravens' Haloti Ngata surprised so many people with his flashy play. In his very first NFL start, this defensive tackle reached up and **intercepted** a Tampa Bay Buccaneers pass. Then he rumbled downfield for 60 yards (55 m) like an out-of-control train.

Haloti has kept the surprises coming ever since—**sacking** quarterbacks and running interceptions back for touchdowns. Ravens coach John Harbaugh jokes that Haloti, with all his flashy plays, might even need a new position such as cornerback. He won't get one, though, because he just does his current job too well.

BIG SEASON
2009

In 2009, Haloti was a key player in a defense that allowed just 93 **rushing yards** (85 m) per game. He helped Baltimore make the playoffs and was rewarded with his first **Pro Bowl** selection.

Haloti (#92) tackles Kansas City Chiefs quarterback Brodie Croyle (#12) during a game in 2009.

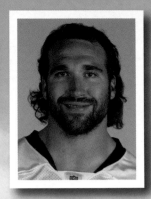

JARED ALLEN #69
MINNESOTA VIKINGS

Position: Defensive End
Born: 4/3/1982 in Dallas, Texas
Height: 6' 6" (1.98 m)

Weight: 270 pounds (122 kg)
College: Idaho State
Pro Bowls: 3

Jared Allen excelled in many different sports as a kid. "In T-ball," remembers his mother, "he would hit a home run every time. In soccer, he would play the entire field."

Unfortunately for NFL quarterbacks, Jared chose football over baseball and soccer. Since he entered the league in 2004, the ferocious defensive end has been a nightmare for quarterbacks.

A backup at first, Jared quickly became a starter after getting four sacks in his first seven games. By 2007, he was the league leader in sacks. Today, opponents often send two or even three players to block him. It's the only way to keep their passers safe.

BIG GAME
October 5, 2009

Jared's best game came in a 30-23 win over the Green Bay Packers. Jared caused a **fumble**, scored a **safety**, and took part in five sacks of Green Bay quarterback Aaron Rodgers.

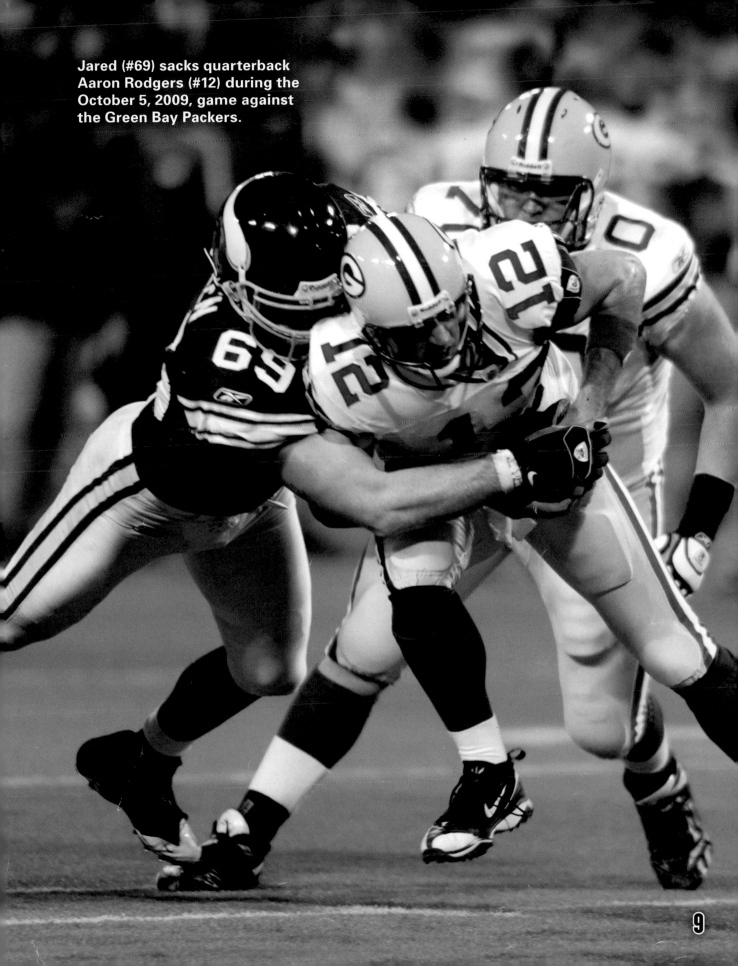

Jared (#69) sacks quarterback Aaron Rodgers (#12) during the October 5, 2009, game against the Green Bay Packers.

DWIGHT FREENEY #93
INDIANAPOLIS COLTS

Position: Defensive End
Born: 2/19/1980 in Hartford, Connecticut
Height: 6' 1" (1.85 m)

Weight: 268 pounds (121 kg)
College: Syracuse
Pro Bowls: 5

Among the Indianapolis Colts, it's quarterback Peyton Manning and the **offense** that get the most attention. The defense, however, has been just as important to their success. A big key to that defense is Dwight Freeney.

Dwight was a latecomer to football. A soccer goalkeeper in high school, he switched sports when the football coach noticed his blazing speed. His incredible quickness is still one of this defensive end's biggest weapons. Using it, he spins past bigger, taller players to get to opposing passers.

How dangerous is Dwight to quarterbacks? Dangerous enough that he has to tone down his game during practice. His coaches frequently remind him, "Don't touch Peyton!"

BIG SEASON
2009

In 2009, Dwight led the Colts with 13.5 sacks and helped Indianapolis to an appearance in Super Bowl XLIV (44) against the New Orleans Saints.

Dwight (# 93) runs around Jacksonville Jaguars tight end Greg Estandia (#83) in the Colts' 2009 season-opening game.

ELVIS DUMERVIL #92
DENVER BRONCOS

Position: Linebacker
Born: 1/19/1984 in Miami, Florida
Height: 5' 11" (1.80 m)

Weight: 248 pounds (112 kg)
College: Louisville
Pro Bowls: 1

Most kids dream about becoming a quarterback. Elvis Dumervil was different, however. Growing up in southern Florida, he dreamed about sacking quarterbacks, not being one. His idols were his older brothers—all defensive players in high school—and legendary pro linebacker Derrick Thomas of the Kansas City Chiefs.

The **All-Pro** linebacker still dreams about sacks. "I love what I do," Elvis says. "I go into every game licking my chops." Elvis doesn't just love the job, he's a master at it. Explosive speed and long arms help him get past **offensive linemen** to tackle a quarterback or knock the ball loose. "There's no better feeling than getting a sack and a **forced fumble**," Elvis says.

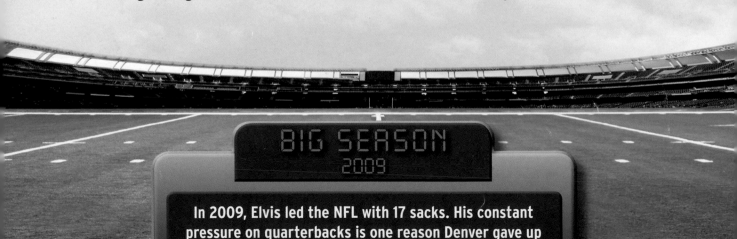

BIG SEASON
2009

In 2009, Elvis led the NFL with 17 sacks. His constant pressure on quarterbacks is one reason Denver gave up fewer **passing yards** than all but 2 of the NFL's 32 teams.

Elvis (#92) sacks quarterback Tony Romo (#9) in a game against the Dallas Cowboys in 2009.

PATRICK WILLIS #52
SAN FRANCISCO 49ERS

Position: Linebacker
Born: 1/25/1985 in Bruceton, Tennessee
Height: 6' 1" (1.85 m)

Weight: 240 pounds (109 kg)
College: Mississippi
Pro Bowls: 3

Patrick Willis has been a "tackling machine" since his first NFL game in 2007. He wowed San Francisco's coaches with nine **solo tackles**. They were so impressed that they kept this amazing linebacker in the game for every single defensive play that season. He was too good to take off the field. By the end of the year, Patrick had taken part in an incredible 174 tackles—the most in the league. In 2009, he again was the NFL's tackle leader. He also had three interceptions—a career best.

Patrick has made it to the Pro Bowl in each of his first three seasons. Still, his coaches think that he can get even better. "There's so much more he can do," says head coach Mike Singletary. "It's amazing to me a guy can have that much ability as a linebacker."

BIG GAME
October 4, 2009

Patrick had a huge role in San Francisco's 35-0 win over the St. Louis Rams. He had 8 tackles, 2.5 sacks, and returned an interception 23 yards (21 m) for a touchdown.

Patrick (#52) gets ready to make a tackle in the October 4, 2009, game against the St. Louis Rams.

DARRELLE REVIS #24
NEW YORK JETS

Position: Cornerback
Born: 7/14/1985 in Aliquippa, Pennsylvania
Height: 5' 11" (1.80 m)

Weight: 198 pounds (90 kg)
College: Pittsburgh
Pro Bowls: 2

Before a play even begins, Darrelle is already at work. He stands **menacingly** at the **line of scrimmage**, staring at the receiver he will cover. "I want to let him know I'm waiting for him," says Darrelle.

That's a scary thought for receivers, since Darrelle makes it nearly impossible for them to catch passes. This incredible cornerback can leap as high and run as fast as the league's best receivers. He's also incredibly strong. The strength comes from off-season weight training that includes lifting monster truck tires.

Preparation is another reason Darrelle is so tough. He spends hours and hours studying **game film**. Before the whistle blows, he already knows all his opponents' weaknesses.

BIG GAME
JANUARY 9, 2010

In the Jets' 24–14 playoff win against the Cincinnati Bengals, Darrelle matched up against Chad Ochocinco, the Bengals' star receiver. Darrelle hounded Chad all game long, allowing him to make just 2 catches for a measly 28 yards (26 m).

Darrelle (#24) defends against Chad Ochocinco (#85) in the January 9, 2010, game against the Cincinnati Bengals.

CHARLES WOODSON #21
GREEN BAY PACKERS

Position: Cornerback
Born: 10/7/1976 in Fremont, Ohio
Height: 6' 1" (1.85 m)

Weight: 202 pounds (92 kg)
College: Michigan
Pro Bowls: 6

Charles's childhood fantasy was winning the Heisman Trophy, college football's highest award. By college, however, it seemed an unlikely dream. Charles played defense, and only offensive players ever seemed to win the Heisman.

In 1997, however, he became the first defender to win the award. He awed voters with his ability to shut down offenses by intercepting passes and forcing fumbles.

The same skills have made him one of the NFL's great cornerbacks. Even if Charles can't stop a receiver from making the catch, he can still break up the play. Often he uses his special move—the slash-and-strip. This is when Charles swings his arms down onto a receiver's hands to knock the ball loose.

BIG SEASON
2009

In 2009, Charles was voted NFL Defensive Player of the Year. He led the league with 9 interceptions, returning 3 of them for touchdowns. He also forced 4 fumbles and made 74 tackles.

Charles returns an interception against the Cleveland Browns in a 2009 game.

DARREN SHARPER #42
NEW ORLEANS SAINTS

Position: Safety
Born: 11/3/1975 in Richmond, Virginia
Height: 6′ 2″ (1.88 m)

Weight: 210 pounds (95 kg)
College: William & Mary
Pro Bowls: 5

For NFL teams, safety is a critical position. As the last defender downfield, a safety protects the **end zone**. Mistakes can easily mean touchdowns.

Darren Sharper rarely makes mistakes. Using a combination of speed, strength, and smarts, he has excelled at the position for three different teams. After making Pro Bowls with the Green Bay Packers and the Minnesota Vikings, he joined the New Orleans Saints in 2009.

Darren began a dream season with five interceptions in his first four games. He went on to make nine interceptions while gaining **376 interception return yards** (344 m)—an NFL record. Even better, he played a key role in helping the Saints to victory in Super Bowl XLIV (44).

BIG PLAY
October 4, 2009

During this playoff game against the New York Jets, Darren intercepted a pass by quarterback Mark Sanchez and ran it back for a 99-yard (91-m) touchdown. It was the longest interception return in the Saints' history and helped New Orleans to a 24-10 win.

Darren celebrates his interception during the October 4, 2009, game against the New York Jets.

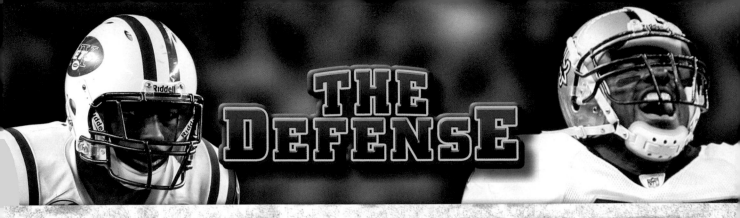

THE DEFENSE

The defense is an important part of any football team. The players who make up the defense are responsible for stopping the other team from scoring. Here's a look at what they do, as well as an example of how they line up on the field.

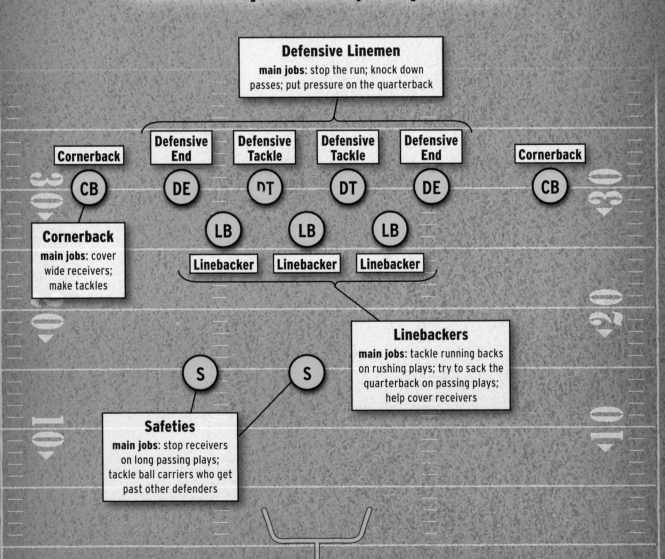

Defensive Linemen
main jobs: stop the run; knock down passes; put pressure on the quarterback

Cornerback
Defensive End DE
Defensive Tackle DT
Defensive Tackle DT
Defensive End DE
Cornerback

CB — CB

LB LB LB

Cornerback
main jobs: cover wide receivers; make tackles

Linebacker Linebacker Linebacker

Linebackers
main jobs: tackle running backs on rushing plays; try to sack the quarterback on passing plays; help cover receivers

S   S

Safeties
main jobs: stop receivers on long passing plays; tackle ball carriers who get past other defenders

END ZONE

GLOSSARY

All-Pro (AWL-PROH) a player who is voted one of the best of the league at his position

cornerbacks (KOR-nur-baks) defensive players who have the job of covering the other team's receivers

defense (DEE-fenss) the part of a team that has the job of stopping the other team from scoring

defensive line (di-FENSS-iv LINE) the group of players (defensive tackles and defensive ends) at the line of scrimmage who try to pressure the quarterback and tackle running backs

end zone (END ZOHN) the area at either end of a football field where touchdowns are scored

forced fumble (FORSST FUHM-buhl) a fumble that is caused by the actions of a defensive player

fumble (FUHM-buhl) a ball that is dropped or lost by the player who has it

game film (GAME FILM) recordings of games already played; they are used by players to study the skills and strategies of their opponents

intercepted (*in*-tur-SEP-tid) caught a pass meant for a player on the other team

interception return yards (*in*-tur-SEP-shuhn ri-TURN YARDZ) yards gained by a defensive player after intercepting a pass

line of scrimmage (LINE UHV SKRIM-ij) an imaginary line across the field where the ball is put at the beginning of a play

linebackers (LINE-*bak*-urz) defensive players who line up behind the line of scrimmage, make tackles, and put pressure on quarterbacks

menacingly (MEN-iss-ing-lee) in a scary way

offense (AW-fenss) the players on a football team whose job it is to score

offensive linemen (AW-fenss-iv LINE-men) the group of players (tackles, guards, and a center) at the line of scrimmage who block for running backs and work to protect the quarterback

passing yards (PASS-ing YARDZ) yards gained on plays in which the ball is passed

Pro Bowl (PROH BOHL) the NFL's all-star game for its very best players

receivers (ri-SEE-vurz) players who catch passes

running backs (RUHN-ing BAKS) players who carry the ball on running plays

rushing yards (RUHSH-ing YARDZ) yards gained on plays in which the ball is run

sacking (SAK-ing) tackling a quarterback behind the line of scrimmage

safeties (SAYF-teez) defensive players who line up farthest behind the line of scrimmage, cover receivers, and tackle ball carriers who get past other defensive players

safety (SAYF-tee) a play in which an offensive player is tackled in his own end zone, resulting in two points for the defensive team

solo tackles (SOH-loh TAK-uhlz) tackles made by a single player

BIBLIOGRAPHY

Crumpacker, John. "Willis Only Gets Better." *San Francisco Chronicle* (December 29, 2009).

Jensen, Sean. "New Minnesota Viking Jared Allen Is Living Large and Small." *Saint Paul Pioneer Press* (April 27, 2008).

Silver, Michael. "He Puts the D in Indy." *Sports Illustrated* (October 17, 2005).

Zillgitt, Jeff. "With 'Brick' on Shoulder, Dumervil Pounds QBs for Broncos." *USA Today* (July 31, 2008).

READ MORE

Holden, Stephen. *Football: Rushing and Tackling.* New York: Children's Press (2000).

Sandler, Michael. *Drew Brees and the New Orleans Saints: Super Bowl XLIV (Super Bowl Superstars).* New York: Bearport (2011).

Sandler, Michael. *Peyton Manning and the Indianapolis Colts: Super Bowl XLI (Super Bowl Superstars).* New York: Bearport (2008).

LEARN MORE ONLINE

To learn more about the NFL's stars of the defense, visit
www.bearportpublishing.com/FootballORama

INDEX